Black Sheep

Black Sheep

Dare to Live an Audacious Life

Joe Small

Library of Congress Control Number: 2023913104
ISBN: Hardcover   979-8-3694-0325-9
                     Softcover   979-8-3694-0326-6
                     eBook   979-8-3694-0324-2

Print information available on the last page.

Rev. date: 07/17/2023

To order additional copies of this book, contact:
Xlibris
844-714-8691
www.Xlibris.com
Orders@Xlibris.com
850946

Contents

Introduction

Since the beginning of time, there has been a hierarchy that rules both our conscious and our subconscious. This hierarchy is one that somehow determines what is valuable in life. People, places, things, and all of nature are a part of this. You can see this illustrated even from the creation of the world where God was creating our universe. There is a reason for the order in which He did things. There are no coincidences in His actions. It is not to say that this hierarchy is right or wrong, but it is important that we acknowledge it. Once we do, there are simple yet profound truths that will unlock potential in many of our lives. It's important to realize God doesn't make mistakes.

You may be thinking, "Great. Another self-help book." Look, I get it. I am always skeptical at first about opening a book and investing my time. I usually think the author must live in an ivory tower and probably hasn't put his money where his mouth is. Or, as kids in East Vegas, where I was raised, say, "This guy is writing checks his body can't cash." As you read how transparent, real, raw, and even funny this book is, you will know I have lived this stuff. I *am* a black sheep, and I think you might agree with that by the end of our journey together, and spoiler alert, don't tell anyone just yet; you might be a black sheep yourself.

Throughout this short yet impactful book, we are going to look at what the Bible calls "the least of these," which means those the world has seemingly overlooked. Yet even though we all go through things, somewhere, somehow in our society, we have decided to focus on the things that divide us rather than the things that unify us. We have far more in common with one another than we have differences.

What I will be sharing with you is stuff that all of us go through. Not a single person has walked the face of the earth and remained untouched by things such as abuse, poverty, war, hunger, ego issues, and so much more we will get into shortly. But time and time again, God uses the people who the world has either outright rejected or have been overlooked. It is *these* individuals who God uses to bring about revolutionary change. It's these individuals who were looked at as out of the ordinary that God, time and time again throughout the history of this planet, continues to use and shape the world we live in.

These individuals who are overlooked or ignored are not just biblical but are found in our everyday lives. There is, without a doubt, one in every home, workplace, and group of friends. They are the individuals who are a part of the group but, for some reason or another, have been looked at as an outcast. Sometimes, that reason is that someone finds that person a bit annoying. Other times, it is because that individual made a mistake in their past. Sometimes, it is because they simply are the newest part of the social group. What is wild is that, at times, some groups don't even know that they are ostracizing this individual, and if that individual leaves that group, the group finds a new person to take on that role.

Odds are, if you are reading this book, you have been this person at some point in time, or you have felt like the one who has been left out. You have felt as if others feel a certain way about you. It is important to know that you are not alone! Nearly all of us over the course of our lives have felt this way. Sure, some have felt it more deeply than others, but it is something that we can all relate to. Throughout this book, you will be reminded of God's promises and that they never fail. No matter how difficult things might be in your life, He sees you, and He uses all things for good.

The purpose of this book is to educate and inform us regarding the black sheep's role in society. The goal is to encourage and empower those that have felt left behind. Raising awareness will also raise the level of empathy for those that battle this stigma. We are going to dig into the individuals throughout history who have dealt with this and have overcome it and become legends. We will look at individuals not just in the Bible but also throughout history and even a bit of pop culture. By accomplishing all of this, not only will people who have felt the way we do, be impacted, but it will also help leaders of organizations recognize these individuals and begin to utilize them at a much greater capacity. Doing so will benefit not only organizations but the black sheep themselves.

You will notice at the end of each chapter, there is a place for you to engage. The heart behind this is that this technique of stopping and pausing, connect with the heart of what you read, being able to explain how you are going to use what connected with you as a positive force for change,and finally praying and meditating are all a part of what has healed this Black Sheep. Reading, writing out thoughts or ideas or emotions or epiphanies, praying and meditating are crucial things that I have found helped me to cope with the trauma that life brings.

Join me on this journey. Let's change the narrative around the black sheep, discover more about our unlimited potential, and together! I believe by the time we end our journey together, we will realize all of us have far more in common than we could have ever imagined, so welcome to *Black Sheep*.

Chapter 1

What the Sheep?

For those of us living in our modern world, the concept of shepherding is way outside of the lens through which we see the world. Most of us wouldn't have the slightest clue as to how to begin shepherding. Not only that, but we certainly wouldn't have any idea of which sheep would be considered more valuable or less valuable. We would just be knee-deep in wool, wondering how in the world we get rid of it. Think about it. Here is one of the crazy things about sheep: while most of us couldn't pick a sheep over a lamb or ram or deer if our lives depended on it, shepherds can. Shepherds know every intimate detail of every member of their flock—every scratch, bruise, different eye color, literally anything. Shepherds are meticulous in how they tend to their flock. Why? Because they love them. They value them. It is the sheep that feed the shepherd, keep the shepherd warm, and keep the shepherd active. If you still don't believe me about how obsessed shepherds are with their sheep, even today, when we can't fall asleep, we are told to count sheep! Sheep are a big deal in our world!

There are many references to what a black sheep is. Some will say that a black sheep is an oddball member of a family. Everyone has a "crazy" uncle, aunt, *tio*, or *tia*. You know the person I'm talking about.

That person who makes decisions that make you go, "Huh, I wouldn't have done that, but alright," and you shrug your shoulders and go about your life. You love them, and they add to your life, but there's no doubt they are unique. They are the ones who, at every family gathering, you can't wait to show up because then, it's a party! And everyone knows there isn't a party like a black sheep party because a black sheep party doesn't stop!

But I want us to dive into this concept and really sink our teeth into it because, in the end, we will all be better for it. There is more to "black sheep-ness" than just it being an idiom. There is something significant here, something powerful that if we grasp it, we can begin to put the black sheep to work in the areas of their strengths, and our life and world become a better place.

Historically, the black sheep phrase can be traced back to the sixteenth century. During this period of time, the color of the sheep's wool, if dark, was considered undesirable. Everyone wanted white wool. The black sheep couldn't create white wool; it could only produce black wool. It is of no fault of its own. The black fleece was caused by a recessive gene. However, it happened. There was a stigma attached to this sheep that was different from the others. The black sheep brought shame to its flock. Black sheep never asked to be different. They never asked to be unique or to stand out. They were born that way. The black sheep would much rather fit in with its family and friends.

By the eighteenth century, the legend of the black sheep had grown. The black sheep had gone from being just an inconvenience to it being considered evil. Quite a jump, if you ask me, but people believed that the black sheep were somehow, some way, stricken by the devil himself. That's right, folks. People in the eighteenth century had racist tendencies like some today. Wild, right? Because I'm sure the devil just one day was hanging around hell and thought to himself, "Diablo, you know what's really ticking me off? *Sheep*. Let's go ahead and smite a sheep every now and then and make them black just to show them who's boss."

Imagine this: it's the year 1650, and you're blessed to be a shepherd with a fair to quite fair-sized flock. One of your sheep starts having babies. You're sitting there with your brother Jethro trying to deliver these sheep babies. They start coming out all willy-nilly, one after another. Then, all of a sudden, one comes out, and gasps! "What in tarnation is that? A black sheep baby? Oh, my lucky stars! I have never seen anything like this," you think. "Surely this rare sheep must be special and valuable because of its uniqueness." You begin parading it in front of the other sheep, but a strange reaction is coming up. The other sheep aren't celebrating the black sheep but are starting to distance themselves, laughing at the black sheep, and refusing to accept the black sheep into any part of their world.

Upon seeing this reaction and learning from fellow shepherds, your region with the black sheep is a sign of some "curse." You immediately rip your loincloths and begin to just sit in ashes because El Diablo has just sent you a "gift" from the pit of Hades. Shame comes upon your family. You have to move to a less-than-desirable grazing area with no shade, except that which is coming from your wife for even you getting wrapped into the sheep business, to begin with. That's how preposterous it all is!

But is it that preposterous? Flash forward to our world today. I can guarantee that in every group, family, tribe, circle, or wherever people regularly gather with a relationship, there is a black sheep. You may not talk about it openly, but you better believe they are there. They are the person who may be bad with money. They may be the person who you can't bring to specific family events because you are afraid they may make a scene. They are the ones who make you uncomfortable at times for some reason, valid or not.

In every boardroom, there is a black sheep—the one who comes up with ideas so outrageous it makes you think they had to have been on a bender worthy of any frat house during pledge week. But more times than not, that crazy son of a sheep's idea works out and saves the day.

The black sheep is the person who you talk about but never talk to. The black sheep is the person who wears their hat backward. The black sheep is the one who says what everyone else is thinking but is too afraid to say it. The black sheep seemingly has no filter at times. The black sheep is messy. The black sheep is the one who gets things done but done in their way, not yours. The black sheep is the one who is willing to go out on a limb without support, and they are comfortable there because, honestly, it's all they know. The black sheep is the one who is creative beyond belief. The black sheep is the athlete who comes off just naturally better than everyone else for some reason. The black sheep does things just flat-out differently. The black sheep is loyal to its very core. The black sheep is empathetic. The black sheep could be artistic. The black sheep could be incredibly smart. The black sheep is an influencer. The black sheep takes risks others deem far too risky. The black sheep is raw, honest, and transparent.

In recent memory, we've seen the black sheep represented in pop culture through people like Kobe Bryant, Andre Agassi, Serena Williams, Dale Earnhardt, President Barack Obama, Justin Timberlake, Robin Williams, Jimmy Fallon, Jimmy Kimmel, Tom Brady, Jackie Robinson, Michael Phelps, Martin Luther King Jr., and, of course, the hilarious Chris Farley who even made a movie named *Black Sheep*.

Have I laid the "you can change the world" stuff yet? I repeat it because you are truly significant and have a purpose! The list of black sheep who have completely captured our hearts and minds and have changed our world is unending! Throughout the journey of this book, we will grow in understanding of who black sheep are in our lives. We will dive into what black sheep have done and are doing now and what our responsibility as black sheep is in the future. We will also look at areas of our lives that have become unmanageable and how one day at a time, we can truly grow and have our lives transform the world around us. Then we will truly see the *why* of the black sheep—why God has created us this way and why the universe needs us to tap into our given abilities to use as a positive force. Finally, we will look at how we will thrive as a black sheep and live in such an audacious way that it challenges other black sheep to not only accept who they are but also celebrate it.

The thing about black sheep is that all a black sheep wants is to be loved. The black sheep will give you the wool off its back just to fit in. But we live in a world where somehow we started pointing out people's differences and sometimes go to extreme lengths just to make them fell different. Why? Pride? Ego? Maybe fear or insecurities? But damn sure are we quick to point the spotlight at our neighbors difference just so we can coil back into a sense of comfort and fitting in with the crowd.

What is it about us that we are so uncomfortable with ourselves that it's easier to point out someone else's flaws so they don't see ours? And are they even flaws? They are the things that make us who we are. I know that I for one, have made horrific choices in my life and have accepted and fought through the consequences of those actions. Whether it's been a week in a rehab, months in the hospital alone, or in jail for weeks, I am still uniquely me. And for whatever fucking reason, people seem to like me, at times. But seriously, when are we going to stop waiting to live our best life and instead tap into the unique abilities we have been given to better our world.

We sit around hoarding for "end times", well life happens suddenly. Black Sheep know it better than most that life is precious. My first sponsor, whom I love dearly, always tells me life is just moments.

Celebrate the good ones, cast aside the rest. What do you have to lose? What do you have to give? What do you have to gain? Do you Black sheep and do it proud and loud so it inspires another black sheep to get off their ass and do the same. The world needs YOU. One of my favorite black sheep of all time is Kobe Bryant and let me tell you, we all need to be more black mamba/sheep to make this world a better place. Looking back, the toughest moments in my life... Church in Houston trying to get us to "toe the company line" while they hid a sex predator, triggering my ptsd from my abuse, or the hurricane, or almost losing an arm, to multiple jail stints, hospital trips, losing my dad, all of it......... has shaped me into the black sheep that I am.

The cost, at hand, is only the history of the world. Sure, we could sit on the sidelines and let wars and rumors of wars, natural disasters, floating space objects/balloons or whatever scare us into hiding....... STOP get the sheep out there and do you're thing. I promise you, you wont be alone, you wont be scared once you meet the rest of us, and we're gonna have a helluva time living life together! So whether you can black sheep poised, classy and confident like President Obama, or if your black sheepness is as silly as Chris Farley who is probably somewhere in a van down by the river making someone laugh so hard their cotton candy comes out their nose. Never has the world been as scary as it is today. You survived a pandemic, wars, riots, natural disasters and God knows how many Kardashian breakups along the way. You are stronger than you believe, kinder than you know, and more valuable to our world than you could ever understand. So, go on that trip to visit family, go explore and adventure as you were created to do, go see the beauty this world has to offer because there are millions of things out there for black sheep to do and see. Tell the world about your journey and the things you've seen, accomplished, engaged with and lets enjoy each others stories. You're doing the best you can with what you have and you're now going to use it to change our world!

Together, it is time for us to celebrate our differences. *Now* is the time for unity and change. Our world is crying out daily at injustices taking place. Our world needs black sheep now more than ever, so join me on this journey.

S- Stop and pause. Let's take a minute to truly connect with what we read and felt.

_____

H-Heart connection. What is something unique that stood out from the previous section, what touched your heart and why?

_____

E-Explain how you can use this as a positive force for change in your daily life. Write it out.

_____

E-Examine yourself to see if there's anything else you want to write. (Your healing story is what is used to change others. God turns all brokenness to goodness for His purpose)

_____

P-Pray towards your purpose. Pray and meditate. Focus on openness and boldness to use the gifts and talents that make you who you are everyday!

Chapter 2

Joseph

Now this is a story all about how my life got flipped turned upside down, and I'd like to take a minute just to sit right there, and I'd like to tell you how I became the fresh prince of Las Vegas. In east Las Vegas, born and raised on the playground was where I spent most of my days chilling out, maxing, and relaxing all cool and all, shooting some b-ball outside of school when a couple of guys who were up to no good started making trouble in my neighborhood. I got in one little fight, and my mom got scared. All right, you get the point, and I probably just made our legal team nervous about copyright issues. And if you do not get the reference, well, we just can't be friends. You can keep reading the book, but friendship is off the table.

I was blessed to be born into a loving family. Both my parents were military brats, and their dads, my grandpas, were lifelong, highly decorated, and distinguished Air Force members. I grew up on an amazing street where a bunch of kids would get together daily and play outside as long as we could or until the streetlights came on. If you know that reference, you know. Many of those kids I am still friends with and talk with to this day! Shout out, Desert Sun kids.

However, there is one kid and his sister, who I won't reveal the names of here. I will *never* speak to them again. The reason, and I will be open, is because one night at a sleepover, I was sexually abused by both him and his sister. I didn't even speak about it until I was in my thirties because of the trauma and just not knowing how to process it as a kid. I reveal this because I want you to know that if you have this trauma, too, *you are loved*. It was not your fault, and you're not alone! You are stronger than you think and doing better than you feel!

Moving on, I will dive into that topic in a bit. Growing up, I was blessed to be able to try all sorts of different activities. For example, in high school, I lettered in baseball, tennis, and orchestra. I was an athlete who was also musical. Honestly, it angered some people to know how good I was at certain things and how easily they seemed to come to me. Was I the most talented or physically gifted, not by a long shot. But as a black sheep, you understand that certain things just fall right into our wheelhouse, and though it's easy, even we can't explain why it is that way. For years, I couldn't figure out why this made other people mad. It wasn't until much later that I realized that some things I took as easy while others worked diligently to get better.

I know you're thinking, "Look, everyone is a legend in their own eyes." As my sponsor said, "Don't you know who I think I am." There's certainly truth to all of it, but it doesn't change the fact that for a black sheep, certain things come naturally easy. Now, yes, I understand that this seems very Moses-like. If you don't know, in the book of Numbers, the author writes that Moses is the most humble man on the planet. The author of the book of Numbers is Moses himself! It's a hilarious self-gloss! Moses is a black sheep that we will dive into later, but for now, I digress. For years, I was the best at certain things, and let me tell you, "I would let you know it." I am a smack talker from way back!

It took me a while to realize that other people weren't having the fun I had when I was competing and playing games with me. It was the combination of being good and smack-talking that made me unbearable for some to play with. Again, to put all this in perspective, this black sheep is so competitive that my parents would ground me occasionally from competitions. I couldn't play any game that kept score. Winning was all that mattered to me. I wanted to be the best, and it was my driving force. Eventually, I realized that if I was going to have friends, I would need to chill out. I learned to make games within games to challenge myself without telling anyone. To me, this was my normal. I thought everyone was like this, but it turned out not so much. I was different. I was a black sheep.

After I graduated high school, I went to college on a scholarship but didn't feel fulfilled. After two years, I decided to quit and joined an internship program at my church. This was definitely a black sheep moment. Throwing away thousands of dollars of free education money to join an uncredentialed internship. Education is huge in my family, and my family had worked hard to make it accessible, and I decided to do something different. Not one person in my family was in ministry. After the September 11, 2001 attacks on our country, something shifted in my heart. I felt that I wanted to give back and be a part of something that just meant something. Helping young people learn about God seemed to check those boxes for me.

So I dove in. I learned how to preach, write sermons, lead groups, and teach classes. I began learning different instruments and taught myself how to play bass, drums, piano, and guitar. Again, black sheep. Leading people came easily to me because I genuinely love people. I was just myself and tried to lead by example. After spending years in the internship, I met a girl who would later become my wife. Against the advice of our pastors, like the black sheep we are, we left the internship. This was the start of a whole new season of this black sheep's life.

During this season of our life, we got married, moved into a condo, and started our first ministry while working jobs to support ourselves. Things were hard, but we had audacious dreams. We never shared those dreams, and they seemed impossible. One of the reasons it felt impossible was that as we left the internship, the pastors we served under had begun to tell all our old friends to stop talking to us and even ostracize or "blackball" us in ministry circles. We came to find out that it was so bad that some of our best friends weren't just at our wedding party, but they were also told not to attend. While we felt these things were unfair and were incredibly hurt, we always tried to live above the noise, and I believe because we did, God honored that.

While getting married, things grew in our little church plant. Suddenly, a church from Los Angeles came across our names in their search for their youth and young adult pastor. I was known for doing things "unconventionally" but was also known for strong leadership, you know, as black sheep tend to do. I didn't think anything would come of it because, at this point, I didn't have a degree or even a pastoral license.

However, the pastor took a chance on us and offered us our dream position. I left everything I knew in Las Vegas and moved to Santa Clarita, California, to help a campus of a church. The students were amazing, and immediately, a bond was formed between myself and the entire staff.

I ended up spending eight years in Los Angeles. In those eight years, I truly grew up. I moved several times until settling in the San Fernando Valley. I got an amazing basset hound named Romeo and had our first child! Aiden Joseph Small was born in July 2009. It was the best time of my life. Things at the church were flourishing as the youth ministry was growing, the church as a whole was growing, and my family was growing.

I knew we wanted multiple kids, so we kept trying to have another after Aiden. Years went by, and we weren't able to make it happen. Then one day, my wife came and told me we were having another baby. I was overjoyed. However, something happened a few weeks after as she started feeling pain. We ended up losing a baby. Before that time, I had never known the pain of losing a child that you never knew. I didn't know how to tell people or even process what that trauma meant, but I pressed through.

Then, the next year, we got pregnant again. Again, we lost the baby. At this point, I just assumed what I had dreamed of was never meant to be. During this season of my life, I don't know how to describe it, but it felt like a weight was just on me. I felt sad. I felt numb to a lot of things. But I didn't pay much attention to it because it was not like the world was going to slow down. I still had responsibilities to tend to. Little did I know that this was the start of some major mental, emotional, physical, and spiritual battles I was about to face.

Depression is something that isn't really talked about a whole lot in ministry circles, and honestly, not enough in our world as a whole. I was sad like never before, and I had zero clue how to get better. I was not used to losing and certainly not losing a loved one. I felt like there was literally nothing I could do to make the situation any better. I couldn't preach a good sermon, tell a great joke, win some golf tournament, work out more, or anything! At this point in my life, I hadn't had anyone tell me anything really about coping skills, let alone how to utilize them. So I did what I knew, which mostly just meant compartmentalizing things and trying to focus on work.

Nothing I was doing was helping. I would stay up praying and reading, trying to figure things out, and nothing made sense. I am an avid and voracious reader. I read every book I could find on miscarriages and how to deal. I felt a little better, but there it was, still a nagging dull dark cloud that followed me. I couldn't explain it. This is a very uncommon thing for me. I am typically a very upbeat and positive person—a person who laughs all the time—and now, suddenly, I feel like I have been hit by a truck.

I remember my pastor taking me to coffee, trying to figure it out, and I just didn't know. I now know that I was going through major depression. Depression and anxiety are nearly taboo things to discuss in faith circles. While it has improved slightly over the years, it is still not talked about enough. Many of us suffer in silence for lack of knowledge of resources and supports out there that truly save lives!

One of the things that made it even more difficult for this black sheep was even though I was struggling with my emotions, I was still seeing positive things happening in my life and ministry. I was asked to speak at conferences and camps. Things professionally were great. I credit the relationships that I had built with sustaining me during this time. Friends really helped me through this season of my life. During this season—and I do believe life is all about seasons, and the good thing is that seasons change—I didn't know where to turn. But instead of enjoying things, things became monotonous and mundane. I couldn't put my finger on it. Again, I now know that I was battling major depression and anxiety. Then the next year, something began to shift.

S- Stop and pause. Let's take a minute to truly connect with what we read and felt.

_____

H-Heart connection. What is something unique that stood out from the previous section, what touched your heart and why?

_____

E-Explain how you can use this as a positive force for change in your daily life. Write it out.

_____

E-Examine yourself to see if there's anything else you want to write. (Your healing story is what is used to change others. God turns all brokenness to goodness for His purpose)

_____

P-Pray towards your purpose. Pray and meditate. Focus on openness and boldness to use the gifts and talents that make you who you are everyday!

Chapter 3

Winds of Change

My wife came to me again and told me we were pregnant. I chose to keep it quiet this time. Weeks go by, and everything is healthy! Our first girl after two miscarriages. We decided to name her Mila, which is short for Milagros in Spanish, which means miracle. The doctors had told us we probably weren't going to have more kids after the second miscarriage. So Mila was a miracle to us. And for what it's worth, she is the sweetest burst of sunshine you could ever meet. I was still battling mental health challenges, but she and her brother were tremendous bright spots in my life and continue to be to this day.

As the blessing of having Mila was transpiring, things at the church were getting weird. At first, I truly couldn't put my finger on it. I would ask questions, but no one was really giving me any explanations of why things felt so tense and just different around the whole staff and church. As I mentioned earlier, black sheep tend not to be included in circles of communication; often, they are just told the outcome and have to deal with the fallout. After an amazing first six years, the atmosphere changed noticeably.

Without going into too many details, there are allegations of impropriety between a pastor and an assistant. To this day, I have no clue what took place. I have an idea, but it doesn't matter at this point. The whole thing was all bad. What is wild is at this same time, suddenly, a church in Texas became interested in hiring me. The position they wanted me for was to become the executive youth and young adult pastor at a church in Houston. To give perspective, most churches in America aren't bigger than around one hundred people. The church in California I was at was around 1,800 or so. The church in Houston's sanctuary sat ten thousand people. While this may seem preposterous, a black sheep gets used to doors closing and others opening. God has always been faithful to the black sheep. I guarantee you that in the parable of the lost sheep from the book of Matthew in the New Testament, the one sheep for which Jesus leaves the ninety-nine is a black sheep. God always has a way of turning things for good!

To make it even more audacious is that I would be taking over for the pastors who I interned under and had hated that we left the way we did—you remember, the ones who had told all my friends not to go to my wedding. So I went to the interview. Honestly, I was not really expecting anything to come of it because I really had no desire to follow the carnage they were sure to leave behind. But as soon as I landed in Houston, I could feel a welcoming presence. I had dreamed of huge doors being opened, and let me tell you, this building has some of the biggest doors I have ever seen. The sanctuary of the church sits ten thousand people and fills it up pretty well three times on a Sunday. It is incredibly impressive. It is everything I had ever dreamed of on the outside.

Oh, I forgot to tell you that at this point, my wife had pulled me into the bathroom before heading to Houston to show me a pregnancy test, and she was pregnant again! So now I have gone from a family of three to five in a blink of an eye. I need to say my youngest, Lucy, is such a blessing like her sister and brother. Each of them are so unique and wonderfully made. All of this was happening while I was finishing my degree from Life Pacific University in Leadership and Ministry. That's right, twelve years after walking away from a full-ride scholarship, I finally became ordained and went and finished my degree. This is significant because it's a very black sheep thing to do to take sixteen years to finish college. *Sure*, most get called doctorate after that long, but I digress.

Long story short, I accepted the position in Houston despite really knowing no one at all but just stepping out in faith. I chose to leave behind a beautiful group of incredible students, leaders, and friends to start all over in Texas. This was not easy for so many reasons, but it was one that truly felt right in that season. Why did I choose to leave everything and everyone I knew? Because a black sheep is going to be a black sheep when a black sheep wants to, quite frankly. It was a wild season, to say the very least.

However, in the midst of all these tremendously positive things happening, I still hadn't dealt with that cloud of depression and anxiety. By ignoring it, it had actually grown as life threw things my way to multiply that feeling. And it was getting worse and worse! Everything was moving forward in a positive fashion for the most part, or so I thought. What I didn't know was that my life was going to become more complicated than I could ever imagine.

We made a move to Houston, and the "honeymoon" period was great. We found a house to rent near the church. Things started smoothly, but then strange things started to happen. I was asked to hire a staff, and I put together a team to lead two large ministries. A red flag came up when they wouldn't let me hire anyone from LA or anywhere else, for that matter. I thought it was strange that they basically told me who to hire. And you know how much black sheep love getting micromanaged.

It was rough because this was a sign of things to come. I thought I was there to lead a youth and young adult ministry of hundreds, but really, ulterior motives were soon to be revealed.

That all being said, the Houston team that remained was amazing and more than welcome. I say "remained" simply because the pastor I was taking over for had recruited over a dozen of key staff to go with him to Las Vegas and plant a church, leaving me holes all over the place that I couldn't fill from outside sources I knew and trusted but had to be filled in other creative ways. Again the Houston remaining team was truly welcoming, even if the executive team at the church was rough at best. I couldn't even begin to describe southern hospitality, but we saw it firsthand. People who volunteered their time to serve the youth and young adults in any capacity are truly heroes. I don't mean just in church; I mean heroes anywhere. It takes a special black sheep type of person to give up hours of their lives to try and love and support another human being, especially the next generation. So again, both my Houston and LA leadership teams were equally great.

Another huge red flag reared its head when literally a month into moving to Houston, I got told that I also had to jump right in and run a youth camp for about five hundred teenagers. I was originally supposed to attend but more to just get my feet wet than jump into the deep end. But the deep end was because the pastor I replaced decided to move to Vegas early and left me hanging. So here I was in Texas, not really knowing anyone, just moved my entire family while my wife was pregnant (she ended up giving birth three days before camp), but I had to go to the camp because I was leading it.

The team in Houston was good, but dear God, who does that to someone? I know now that I didn't have proper boundaries and pushed back with everything I had. I didn't have boundary-setting tools in my arsenal at this point in my life. As a young pastor, you're told to say yes and amen to just about anything to advance the kingdom of God. It is a terrible leadership flaw that many, *many* churches still employ on their younger staff and leaders today! Submit, honor, stay accountable, and look away while the leader telling you to do this stuff gets away with being some of the most narcissistic individuals you will ever meet. Are all senior leaders in churches like this? No. But a vast majority have become that way because of the rise of the "celebrity pastor culture."

But I digress. I still had that nagging cloud of mental health challenges hanging over me, and I now had kids at home that I was missing, along with a wife in over her head with two newborns and a toddler. So what did this black sheep do? I threw myself into the work, just compartmentalizing and producing. A completely horrific decision, as I was about to find out. Now, I love the process of work. My work ethic is huge for me, and I have the "Mamba mentality" like Kobe Bryant, where sure, I may be talented, but you're not going to outwork me either.

Camp finishes, and the normal routine of ministry, with its highs and lows, goes on. But early on, while I was leading these ministries, all of a sudden, the senior pastor asked if I would be open to having a former youth pastor come down and evaluate the ministry. What is the fruit? Why? We were just getting started, and things were progressing. But of course, I said, "As you wish." *Princess Bride* is another fun reference for you, but that was what I said. This pastor came down and was super friendly. He told me, "No worries, it's just G being G (referring to the senior pastor)."

We go out to lunches and hang out. He sits and hears me speak and seems to love everything we are doing but writes that we need more teams and stuff. Of course, we did. We just got there! No problem, we start implementing everything this man says. Then one day, I was asked to go pick him up from the airport because he had resigned from his own church and was coming to be on our staff again. The only word that he would say to me is, "Vortex. We're creating a vortex." As a weather nerd, I could appreciate that. But that day was the beginning of a new season for this black sheep. This guy had been announced as the new executive pastor to all of our staff.

S- Stop and pause. Let's take a minute to truly connect with what we read and felt.

_____

H-Heart connection. What is something unique that stood out from the previous section, what touched your heart and why?

_____

E-Explain how you can use this as a positive force for change in your daily life. Write it out.

_____

E-Examine yourself to see if there's anything else you want to write. (Your healing story is what is used to change others. God turns all brokenness to goodness for His purpose)

_____

P-Pray towards your purpose. Pray and meditate. Focus on openness and boldness to use the gifts and talents that make you who you are everyday!

Chapter 4

Cap'n Season

Have you ever seen the meme about the kid wearing white shoes? Became a whole thing about people pointing at odd shoes and shouting, "What are those?" It's an insult but done in a sarcastic, humorous way. In the nineties, we would call it cap'n. Lame, sure, but accurate nonetheless. Black sheep are used to this as we get insulted all the time, and usually, it's followed up with "no offense." Most of us black sheep have heard it so much we get pretty good with our words as well. As I have said, I am a smack talker from way back, and I can be one that throws around an insult for the sake of comedy like the best of them. But this next season of my life, I *never* expected it to happen!

At our mega-church in Houston, we had large "staff meetings" weekly. A few songs, and then a pastor would give some leadership lessons. Well, one day, the senior pastor decided he would spice things up a bit and mocked the way I dressed in front of the entire staff. To be fair, I would rock a pink shirt or something unique as an expression of creativity and to create conversation from time to time, so I was used to comments, and I was here for them. But that day, I wasn't wearing anything unusual. I brushed it off and was going to let it go, but for weeks, it would keep happening on random occasions.

I eventually realized he wasn't joking at all. That's the thing about southern hospitality—half the time, you don't know if they're telling you the truth or making fun of you. It's not an obvious thing; it's subtle and honestly pretty terrible. Unless it's a grandma saying "oh bless your heart" which means, dear God only the divine can keep you from being any more dumb, which is flat out hilarious!

One day, I realized that he truly hated the way I dressed. It got to the point that the senior pastor took me shopping (multiple times) and bought new, more expensive clothes so that I would stop "embarrassing him" with how I dressed. Oh, yes, my friends, this actually happened. Not only was it insulting, but he would also say little things like, "Your dad never told you how to dress?" This mother trucker had the glibbest, self-righteous sense of self I had ever seen. At this point, I could start seeing the end of my time in Houston nearing. There was only so much of that a person could take, no matter how nice the church looked on the outside.

You would think this jackwagon of a leader would be done after that, but *no*! After moving on from my clothing, he began to take his focus and ridiculousness out on one student who had moved with us from LA. You see, this young man was an incredible leader who had beat cancer twice and was a real people person. However, due to the treatments, he had to undergo, he was shorter than most people, and his hair was what you would expect of someone who had battled and beat cancer not once but twice. But because of the way he appeared (black sheep), I got called into the pastor's office and told that he was not allowed to be on stage ever again. This was now beginning to piss me off as a black sheep who is fiercely loyal to those they care about. Being a jerkface to me was one thing; doing it to someone I care about is never a good thing. I had had enough! So I asked belligerently, "Why the fuck not?" (As I said, I may be a pastor, but I, at my core, am an East Vegas kid and black sheep so swearing is a part of me.)

After their shock at my blunt and aggressive tone, he said, "He doesn't represent the image we're trying to portray." I swear to my momma, I thought this pastor was making a joke. Turned out not so much. Not only did they not let me have him be on my staff, but he was also not allowed to be on the stage. I was blown away. I mean, what pastors would be so damn judgmental? (It turned out quite a bit, but as a black sheep, I just assumed everyone in ministry was empathetic and at least had decency). There was no way I was being told not to let him play, right? Wrong! They were deadly serious. They mentioned things like, "Well, kids are laughing at him." Seriously? We are this childish? I was beyond myself. I told the senior pastor, "If you don't want him, you tell him because I'm not." Did he? Hell no, like the judgmental coward he was, he didn't have the balls to tell him that. So I had that young man play up until I left, and he was so loved in Htown.

Here was when my depression and anxiety started to get so hard, and my life was becoming unmanageable. It was the beginning of the end of my time in Htown. Now I was being pulled into meetings with the executive pastor to talk about the "future." I was being talked to as if I was a child but, like Princess Elsa says, "I let it go." I acted like I didn't know what they were doing and played their little game for a while, but it was truly taking a toll on me. These meetings became frequent occurrences, and I was being asked, "What's next?" What's next? The audacity of this dude blew me away. I just got here, and I was growing two ministries for him, and now what's next? I just started!

I hadn't even begun, and now we're talking about what's next. It became clear that they were having these meetings with me because they wanted to move my position. The black sheep had reared its head, and they weren't fond of it. Publicly everything was fine, but internally their staff was a dumpster fire. Meetings would take place, then after the meeting, some in stairwells, all the while, they kept saying how much they loved us. What I didn't catch on to at first was the fact that before I had even moved to Texas, that church had made some horrific choices in how it had handled abuses by its staff. I'm not talking about making fun of staff now. We're talking about issues with protecting minors—*that* kind of stuff. You know, the kind of stuff you might want to mention to a guy coming on staff who was bringing his pregnant wife and two young children across the country. But no, black sheep don't get extended that type of courtesy.

Instead, we get handed a crisis and have to black sheep our way out of it. So that's what I did. I chose to love the people there as hard as I could because most of them were victims of this. As fiercely as I tried to love the people, I was also not holding back on giving my opinion on exactly how fucked up this situation was while behind closed doors. The audacity to judge someone's clothes or their stature after cancer, all while hiding behind your state-of-the-art church building from the fact you didn't fire that staff member but let him go lead in another town, is atrocious. Sadly, this isn't the first church to do that, and it won't be the last. Broken people have made broken decisions since the beginning of time. It's why Adam and Eve tried to hide from God after sinning. Same thing, just a different apple.

While I was there trying to do my best and spending honestly most of my time trying to minister to people who were hurting, eventually, I decided that they obviously didn't want me to be their youth pastor. They really wanted the executive pastor's old youth pastor. Even though we were incredibly well-liked by just about every person there, we just didn't fit their mold. Black sheep. The leadership was perplexed at how I was still able to lead despite their best efforts to circumvent that process. My family and I loved so many of the great people there, but for some reason, the leadership just didn't like us. I would joke that everyone had been invited over to the senior pastor's house except me. To this very day, never been. Black sheep. Our kids loved Texas; the school was great with our son, and the daycare at church was basically a giant McDonald's playground, so they were very well taken care of.

It was then that the depression became unbearable. I began to look for ways to cope, but I didn't honestly know how. I reached out to one of the older pastors several times, telling him I didn't feel right. Something was off. This had been going on. Meanwhile, my appendix ruptured, and I have had a lifelong battle with kidney stones. So in the two short years that we were in Texas, I had several medical procedures. The appendix rupturing was wild because of my high pain threshold. I waited days, thinking it was just some stomach bug. Turned out not so much. Also, along the way, my son was having issues at school, and we began to have him checked by doctors. They tell us that Aiden is on the autism spectrum (for whatever that meant) and believe he might have Asperger's and a few other diagnoses.

So here we are at a standoff professionally, as they don't want me to be the youth pastor, but I was so darn likable and hadn't done anything wrong, so they couldn't fire me with cause. Finally, I had enough and decided to say, "OK, I'm fine not being the youth pastor, but what do you want me to do?" I kid you not; it was as if I said some magical words, and all of a sudden, I was their favorite person. They wanted to bring in the youth pastor from the executive pastor's old church—as everyone expected the entire time—but had no idea how to get me out of the way. So I acquiesced, and my mental and emotional health took a beating. Let me stop here and say that I understand that life is all about perspective. I know that I had things pretty well. All I needed to do was shut up and move out of the way, and they would still take care of my family and me. But again, any black sheep will tell you we just aren't built to just sit on the sidelines.

It was at this point that, after not picking up a bottle of alcohol for over a decade, I began to drink. Secretly at first, of course, because we don't do that, right? It's not OK for a Christian to drink. Sure, the Bible talks about wine all the time, but hey, different times, right? Well, turns out I'm not good at the whole drinking thing. For me, one drink is too many, and a thousand is never enough. But I had no context for this because I had never really drunk in the past. Sure, I did at high school parties and in my early college years, but then I stopped and never missed it. Never thought about it until then. I would go to work, have all the "fun" meetings about transition, and play my role, and then at night, after the kids would go to sleep, I would drink alone.

The Big Book of Alcoholics Anonymous says, "Life becomes unmanageable." Let me tell you, I had blown past unmanageable to spiraling out of control. However, like any black sheep worth its salt, I was still pretty darn charismatic and could fool anyone into thinking I was fine. Was I still producing? Yes, but I wasn't myself anymore. I would numb the emotional and mental toll by drinking. I didn't know where to turn. I knew something had to change, but I truly could see no way out of the situation I was in. Then the day came for a friend's wedding that my wife helped plan, and my daughter was going to be the flower girl. That day I was home, and darkness kept creeping in, and I didn't know what to do. On our way to the wedding venue, I stopped at the store and got some alcohol. I honestly couldn't even tell you what it was. There was no part of me that wanted to drink. I desperately wanted to watch my little princess Mila walk down the aisle as a flower girl. I never got that chance. Once I dropped her off, I began drinking in my car because I had nowhere to go and nowhere to be for a few hours. That was when the first blackout that I could remember happened. I woke up in a hospital with an IV in my arm and no clue what had taken place. I heard some great people did a lot that day, and I am forever grateful.

This was the first bottom that this black sheep had felt. I had to take a taxi in hospital clothes to my house. The church didn't know what to do. I was told to stay away from the church and not talk to anyone. Over the next month, they would fly my wife and me to Dallas to meet with a renowned therapist several times. He told me I had severe depression and anxiety. I had been using alcohol to cope with these mental health struggles. We ended up taking several trips to this wonderful therapist who had treated high-level executives and even many hall-of-fame professional athletes. For whatever reason, I signed an agreement that allowed this therapist to share his opinions on my condition with the church in Houston, mostly because if I didn't, I wasn't going to get his help. For someone with anxiety, this was difficult, but I knew that at this point, I needed to be as transparent as possible if I was ever going to heal. The therapist told me that I would be able to recover, but it would take time and loving support.

Over the next few months, I was not allowed to even attend our church at the pastor's request. This made it even more difficult as it isolated us from all the relationships we had built. So many people were confused by the church's decision, and I couldn't tell them what was really happening as I had no desire for them to pick up my offenses, as I knew some of them would certainly do since they are great people. We got called to meet at the school our church ran. You could cut the tension in the room with a knife; it was so thick. The senior pastor and new executive pastor sat across from my wife and me. There was a lot said and questions asked. The one thing that stood out was the senior pastor who had the audacity to tell me, "God told me you're a liar." Now, had I been lying about things and hiding them? Absolutely. But what was the main takeaway from the meetings with my therapist? Seriously? Hell, I could tell you that I am like every other human being in the world and lie. Do I try to be a person of integrity? Absolutely! But when I drink, there is no amount of lies I won't tell to keep going. They said they weren't ready to make a decision and to stay away. At this point, we saw the writing on the wall. They were going to use this as the opportunity to move on from us.

A few more weeks went by with us hanging in limbo, and finally, my wife and I were summoned to the senior pastor's office. They told us that they believed in us and that the ministry was still in our future but not there with them. There it was, the decision we knew was coming. Even though I thought I was prepared, I broke down in tears. I explained that I didn't understand because I had come to them for help and was told, "You need to pray more." Their minds were made up. They also asked me to resign, and if I was willing to do that and also agreed not to speak on some of the horrific things I knew they were hiding for the next six months, they would pay my full salary and benefits. We accepted these terms and went home, not knowing what our future held.

Just like that, everything I had dreamed of, sacrificed for, and worked hard for had been taken away. Do I blame them for their decision? No. I accept full responsibility for the fact that I made decisions that put so many people in bad positions. Do I agree with how they handled things? Not in the least. But none of this changed the fact that now I was unemployed in a city I only knew and people that I could no longer continue relationships with, with a wife and three kids. All my work experience and education were focused specifically on being a pastor. How was I going to provide for my family now? My depression, anxiety, and mind started running faster than Usain Bolt. I couldn't sleep. I didn't know what to do. I started reaching out to family and friends, asking if, in their opinion, someone with my background could do well in their career choice. They were all very kind but didn't really understand why I was asking, and I couldn't find the right words to really explain what I was going through. What I didn't realize was that something crazy was looming on the horizon.

S- Stop and pause. Let's take a minute to truly connect with what we read and felt.

_____

H-Heart connection. What is something unique that stood out from the previous section, what touched your heart and why?

_____

E-Explain how you can use this as a positive force for change in your daily life. Write it out.

_____

E-Examine yourself to see if there's anything else you want to write. (Your healing story is what is used to change others. God turns all brokenness to goodness for His purpose)

_____

P-Pray towards your purpose. Pray and meditate. Focus on openness and boldness to use the gifts and talents that make you who you are everyday!

Chapter 5

Hurricane SZN

Growing up in Las Vegas, a desert, the rain wasn't something you really paid much attention to. Then living in California, it was very similar—storms are few and far between. Texas—totally different story! Houston, in terms of weather, is Satan's armpit. The humidity is stifling, and it rains almost every day. Then when it storms, *it storms*! I had never seen rain like this before; it was beyond wild. Why people settled there, I would never understand. Imagine being a pilgrim or whomever and coming to the Houston area, and for some unknown reason, you decide, "Welp, this is as good as it could get."

Every few years, hurricanes come and basically stop life as you know it, something I was about to find out. Thirty-six inches was what was predicted. That would have been delightful. Fifty-four inches of rain falling from the sky and the wind—oh sweet heaven—the wind! Hurricane Harvey hit just south of us, but then we came to Houston and just hung out like a houseguest that couldn't figure out the cues that it was time to leave. This Vegas boy had hit the store prior to it, hitting and getting the essentials, except milk—you know, that substance kids just love to drink, and I happen to have three of those dairy lovers. Once the flooding receded enough for us to get out to the store, we began to see the devastation. Homes were destroyed, cars totaled, and businesses completely flooded. They only let people into the store three at a time. I got the essentials, water, bread, meat, cheese, and cereal, but we couldn't find milk. Oh, of course, I grabbed alcohol because, at this point, I would come to find out later I had now added PTSD to the list of mental health struggles I was dealing with.

We were incredibly fortunate that our house was at a high point in our neighborhood, so it didn't flood. Also, we were on the same power grid as a fire station, so when our power would go out, it wouldn't take long for it to come back on. I started to realize how bad it was when Anderson Cooper from CNN was reporting from two blocks away from our house. I could still remember walking into my backyard and counting twelve helicopters circling. Some of the helicopters were circling for the news. Some were lowering baskets and rescuing families. One of the fun facts I learned during Hurricane Harvey was that a fridge floats! Who knew?

I have pictures of our kids playing in the rain as we had our own little "Hurricane Party." Thankfully, the kids were so little that they don't remember much of the hurricane. However, the damage Hurricane Harvey did was not just to buildings but also to my mental and emotional state. When I was able to, I would go out and help neighbors and strangers go through a process called "mucking" their homes. They needed to do this to get ready for FEMA to come and evaluate their damages.

I had decided to move back home to Las Vegas, and ironically, my house hit the market the same day Hurricane Harvey hit Houston. Another thing that stood out was that I offered to come to help our church, the place that had asked me to resign, but they asked me to still stay away. I was blown away that they didn't even want my help, but I digress. We began packing and starting the process of moving home, not knowing what the future held. No job, no home, no sense of security. I send my family on to Vegas ahead of me while my mom and I drive. The biggest moving van there is towing our car.

After a several-day trip, we move into my loving in-laws' place, where we will stay for nearly a year and a half. During this time, we struggled to find employment and a sense of stability. My mental health was still rough. I had no clue where to turn. I felt completely lost, nothing made sense, and the joy that was always easy for me to tap into was gone. My secret drinking at this point got out of hand. I had no clue how I was able to hide it for so long, but I did. I hated that I was doing it. I was ashamed, embarrassed, and angry with myself and God.

I wasn't myself, but I didn't know how to pull myself up. I threw myself into being the best husband, dad, uncle, brother, son, and person I could be, but I wasn't willing to stop drinking. For me, at this point, the drinking in my warped mind was something I looked forward to. All the days were the same—drop off kids, drink, sleep, pick up kids, repeat the next day. One cool thing that happened during this season was that my Spanish and cooking skills became awesome. That is the typical black sheep—things could be hell on earth, but somehow, you could still execute some things really well.

I could never understand how I had truly let things get so overwhelming. Losing the career or what I felt at the time was a calling, was devastating. All I wanted to do was help people live their best life and be the best version of themselves. Little did I know at the time, the storm was far from over, it had just begun and yet again, my life was about to be flipped upside down.

S- Stop and pause. Let's take a minute to truly connect with what we read and felt.

_____

H-Heart connection. What is something unique that stood out from the previous section, what touched your heart and why?

_____

E-Explain how you can use this as a positive force for change in your daily life. Write it out.

_____

E-Examine yourself to see if there's anything else you want to write. (Your healing story is what is used to change others. God turns all brokenness to goodness for His purpose)

_____

P-Pray towards your purpose. Pray and meditate. Focus on openness and boldness to use the gifts and talents that make you who you are everyday!

Chapter 6

Jails, Institutions, and Death

Addiction is a destructive force that impacts so many people, not just the one who is battling addiction. Addiction doesn't care about your socioeconomic status. I come from a family that has a history of addiction issues with various individuals and varying degrees of despair. I believe that if you're reading this book, almost all of our families do. The question becomes how your family deals with it. Some families are fine with it and just take it as part of normal life. Some confront it and begin to take steps to eradicate it. Others may sweep it under the rug. You never know what your family does until it comes time to do it.

Well, one day in Vegas, I took my depression meds and drank earlier in the day. Later, I was asked to go get some food from In 'n' Out. If you haven't had In 'n' Out, you haven't truly lived, but that's not the point. The point is that I remember driving to In 'n' Out and ordering, but the next thing that I remember was waking up inside a jail cell by myself. I don't remember ordering a DUI, but that's what I was getting. I had zero recollection of what happened. I didn't know where I was, what I had done, or if I had hurt anyone. It was just me and a blanket that smelled of hot garbage and burnt hair on a concrete bench. Eventually, an officer told me I was arrested for DUI, and I could make a call. This would not be my last phone call from jail. I spent a day in jail and was released in the middle of the night the following night.

I had tremendous family support. I say that because this black sheep felt the support but also could feel the distancing that comes with that level of concern. Turned out that the police found me asleep in my vehicle at an intersection. They had to break the window to get in. I had no recollection of anything. These are things I learned later from reading my case file. All of this was new to me. I mean, sure, I had run-ins with police before, but nothing like this. I had never been arrested up until that point. The closest thing to this was the time during my internship when a few friends, including my wife, had been playing with airsoft guns.

One day, on a breakfast break, we decided to go to get some McDonald's. I picked up a clear airsoft gun and pointed it at my future wife, and told her to get in the car jokingly. Apparently, the joke was not shared with the parents who were dropping their kids off at school that morning who saw that take place. Unbeknown to us, the police had been called. We got through the drive, and there were about six cop cars with police pointing guns at us—us, being ministry school interns learning how to be pastors and serve people. An officer who resembled Alfred E. Newman yanked me out of the car and threw me on the hood of a police car. Guess who was singled out here? You guessed it. The black sheep. Eventually, they figured out that I was not taking hostages with a clear gun but not before they locked down several area schools in the scare. Yep, that was me, "black sheeping" so hard that schools are getting locked down. Oh ho ho, the meeting I had with the pastor after that was not fun at all! After I pled guilty and did everything the judge asked in terms of courses, I eventually found my way into rehab.

Now, there was some time here when things got really bad. This included me, at one point, being put on a seventy-two-hour hold and sent to a psychiatric ward. I am not going to dive deep into those details because I don't want to come across as glorifying the darkest of dark seasons but rest assured, we will touch upon them at the end, as I know many can relate. Things between myself and my wife became tense, relationships with family became strained, and everything was at the absolute worst place you could imagine. I didn't know what the next day held, let alone any future I had in any relationship. Depression was winning, and I was absolutely exhausted. In the patient rehab for the first time was where I ended up.

I remember sitting in the living room of a strange house, thinking, "How the hell did I end up here?" Just a few years ago, I was living my dreams, and now I had been to jail and now rehab. Who am I? What am I doing with my life? The thirty days that I was away from my family was the hardest part of my entire life up to that point. I said that having been through countless surgeries, church backstabbing, and even the day in jail. Not being able to see my kids was torture that I had to push through. It took me a few days, but eventually, I threw myself all into rehabilitation. I learned much about myself that I never knew. I had spent years focusing on meeting others' needs, and all the while, I had neglected my own. I realized that if I didn't get it together, the only place left that I hadn't been to was the morgue. This reality drives me to this day.

After I got out of rehab, I got a job working for the city, running youth sports and aquatics. I enjoyed being able to give back. I had a staff, and things were starting to get back to what I felt was a normal life. However, there was so much work to be done in the important relationships that I had in my life. Just because I was healing didn't mean the people who stood by me during this time had gone through the same healing process. I didn't understand this at the time, and it was difficult for anyone who was in recovery. A year went by, and things were slowly improving on multiple fronts. Some relationships had been salvaged and were becoming stronger than ever, while some relationships came to a seasonal end. I think this is an important thing to understand, that some relationships come into your life only for a season and some for a reason. There are others that come into your life that are lifelong road dogs if you will. You see, black sheep are loyal. Black sheep are built for tough seasons. Black sheep are built to weather any storm. Some sheep aren't built that way, and that's fine, but I don't understand those sheep. I wish I could tell you that this was the end of all the bad things that happened, but we're just getting to some juicy parts—parts that literally almost kill me.

S- Stop and pause. Let's take a minute to truly connect with what we read and felt.

_____

H-Heart connection. What is something unique that stood out from the previous section, what touched your heart and why?

_____

E-Explain how you can use this as a positive force for change in your daily life. Write it out.

_____

E-Examine yourself to see if there's anything else you want to write. (Your healing story is what is used to change others. God turns all brokenness to goodness for His purpose)

_____

P-Pray towards your purpose. Pray and meditate. Focus on openness and boldness to use the gifts and talents that make you who you are everyday!

Chapter 7

Sorry, We Almost Killed You

Remember I mentioned kidney stones earlier? Well, now they are starting to show up with much bigger kidney stone friends requiring procedures. Having grown up with kidney stone issues, I have what you would call a ridiculously high pain threshold. This has been both a good and bad thing for me over the years. Good in that without it, I'm not sure I would still be here. Bad in that sometimes, between my pain threshold and my stubborn black sheepness, I come close to dying before I go to a doctor. I'm not one of those who head to the emergency room thinking they had a heart attack only to find out it was gas. As I was coming to the close of swim season for the city, I started to have that nagging pain that I'd come to know from my left kidney. I tried to keep pushing through and drinking water, you know, because I'm a black sheep, and at times, I'm just stupid. So the pain finally got so bad I had to leave for the hospital.

The hospital I went to, of course, didn't have a urology department yet, so they took me by ambulance across town. By this time, my body had begun doing something new. I was shaking like a space shuttle from a third-world country. I couldn't seem to get my body to stop shaking, and honestly, it was pissing me off. Not only was I in pain, but now I got the wiggles. Really? I swear my body hates me, but I digress. They rushed me into surgery only to have me wake up in a room, and they told me they couldn't do the kidney procedure because my body had now gone septic. I didn't know what that meant, but I soon learned it was not good. I had an infection that had now spread to my lungs. An alarm went off, and all of a sudden, a billion doctors and nurses rushed into my room.

Hazy is what I would call my recollection of the next several days. They put me in PCU for four days before moving me to a monster room with a killer view. This was where I started to remember things. Some doctor who specialized in infectious diseases came in and said, "Wow, nice room. This is the sorry-we-almost-killed-you room." We got to laughing and giggling like school kids, but then I thought what the fruit just happened? Turned out that infection nearly got to my heart, and if so, as Bugs Bunny would say, "That's all, folks." So now I had overcome an infection, but I still had a kidney stone the size of a Buick inside me. So a few weeks later, I got to try again to get this bad boy out of me. This time, it worked—hooray!

What I didn't realize was that cross-addiction is a real thing, and also being knocked out, or put under, in medical terms, as many times as I have, has put my body into extreme trauma response. I started going back to work and trying to get my life back. But addiction doesn't take sympathy time off. After a while, I started going back to the old coping mechanisms instead of utilizing the tools I had acquired in rehab. I started hiding my drinking again. Do I want to drink? Hell no. But I couldn't seem to stop myself. For years of being a stubborn black sheep, I had prided myself on my self-will and determination. My pride and ego probably caused it to go on longer than it should have. Again, one drink was too much, and one thousand is never enough. I had fallen into the same old patterns again. This time it would leave a mark.

Things at work were rough. While my department head was tremendous, my immediate boss was impossible to work for. I started having flashbacks to my last church and how they treated me. This boss would belittle me all the same. This boss would give me something to do with no instruction. I would kill it, but the boss would find something wrong and make me redo it just because. You know, one of those types of bosses. Then came the day they told me that they were going to switch my role. I was no longer going to be over youth sports; I got to instead do all the administrative functions of the office. For any black sheep, this is a death sentence. I'm a peacock—you got to let me fly! I didn't know what to do. Again, I started resorting to my same bad coping skills, a.k.a. drinking.

During this period of time, my marriage crumbled for various reasons. While it hurt, not being with my kids was the thing that absolutely killed me. As a black sheep, all I want is to belong. All I want is to be part of the family, and at this point, I wasn't healthy enough to do that. I got so bad that I missed one of my kid's birthdays. I felt horrible.

How could I do that to them? This isn't me! But at that time, it was. The next several weeks were a whirlwind of bad decisions. I kept drinking. I was completely out of control. One day, after a night of heavy drinking, I got pulled over. Was I drunk at the time? No. But it didn't matter. I was taken to the county for failure to maintain a lane. They charged me with another DUI. I spent two days in jail this time, all the while thinking, "What am I doing with my life?" Eventually, they dropped the charges because I wasn't under the influence. But the damage was still done.

My incredible aunt and uncle picked me up and took care of me. Throughout this season, while one side of my family was shunning me, another side embraced me. The kindness of my grandparents, aunt, uncle, and cousins was truly life-saving. But the difficulty from the other side of the family was so painful. Let me just take a moment and tell you that as a black sheep, all you desire is to fit in and be loved. As the black sheep, I understand that we can be a bit much, but what I don't understand is turning your back on family. I say this because, again, storms reveal true character. Out of the abundance of the heart, the mouth speaks. So imagine your heart being a cup. Whenever you get shaken by a storm, all of a sudden, whatever is in your cup starts to spill out. In the notebook that I took to rehab, I wrote one goal: to be able to spend Thanksgiving with my family. I went through rehab and was released in time, but my family, the ones I desperately wanted love and approval from, had decided that my family and I were not welcome at the family thanksgiving. I was devastated. At this point, I now had pastors and family turning away from me in moments when I truly needed them the most. It is something that this black sheep continues to work through in therapy. The damage a black sheep who chooses to handle life the way I had at this point does to his family is tremendous.

Then came the day I got home and found a bottle of alcohol I had stashed at some point. That day I drank so much that I ran into a wall with my left arm. I woke up with my arm swelled two to three times its normal size and growing. My wife ordered me an Uber to take me to the hospital. The ER doctor had no clue what the issue was. There were no broken bones, but the swelling kept getting worse. They admitted me into the hospital. Miraculously, the admitting doctor was a war veteran who had seen this type of injury before. Compartment syndrome is what it is called. It typically takes place in car accidents or in war. It is where a part of one of your extremities experiences trauma, and the swelling stays in one compartment of that extremity. If not quickly taken care of, people lose limbs.

The doctor called in a specialist, and they rushed me into surgery, where they opened up my arm and placed a wound vac on it. I would stay in the hospital for several weeks and would have to undergo several more procedures. Going into the surgery, the doctor laid out all the options saying that I might lose the arm, I might lose all mobility, or the best case scenario was I had a gnarly scar and would regain most of my functionality. I told him to do whatever he could, but I would prefer not to end up on a tripod. Thankfully, it went as well as it could, and today, I have nearly full mobility with little pain in my left arm.

Why am I going into this much detail early on about so many struggles? For the simple fact that we live in a world that glorifies life's highlights. We live in a day in age where everyone posts the most filtered version of their best moments on social media platforms, pretending that is all their life is about. I am here to tell you that life is fun and full of great adventure, absolutely. But just as there are plenty of mountain tops, there are also equally as many valleys. It is in those valleys of life that grass grows, and a black sheep begins to feed itself to give it the strength to get to those very mountain tops we all desire to reach!

Now at this point we are going to shift and begin to look at several historical people that are brought up in many ancient writings. After looking at some of their life lessons, which are incredibly significant, I will wrap a bow on this bad boy and even let you know where this black sheep's life is at personally as I share my journey. Again all of this is in hopes of shining a light on the reality that black sheep have been around since the beginning of time. Since civilization began, black sheep have made tremendous impacts on our world. My belief is that as I share my story and point out other black sheep, YOU will begin to look inside and see the gifts you have been given. It is those gifts that our world needs in such an uncertain and wild time. While many individuals use their talents to benefit only themselves, black sheep have the uncanny ability to use their lives to truly benefit their families, their communities, and the world at large.

So let's dive in as we continue to look at black sheep and we also continue to examine our own lives. I hope the tools at the end of each chapter will only spark a desire within you to further your personal growth time daily. It truly is a discipline that has changed my life for the better and allowed me to tap into the best parts of me. By taking just a few moments daily to check in with myself and my higher power that I call God, it unlocks my ability to be more present, productive and more wise throughout the day. This only leads to a sense of fulfillment and joy which battles back and works to replace my depression, anxiety, and more. My belief and hope is that it will do the same for you, and in turn will benefit all of us.

S- Stop and pause. Let's take a minute to truly connect with what we read and felt.

_____

H-Heart connection. What is something unique that stood out from the previous section, what touched your heart and why?

_____

E-Explain how you can use this as a positive force for change in your daily life. Write it out.

_____

E-Examine yourself to see if there's anything else you want to write. (Your healing story is what is used to change others. God turns all brokenness to goodness for His purpose)

_____

P-Pray towards your purpose. Pray and meditate. Focus on openness and boldness to use the gifts and talents that make you who you are everyday!

Chapter 8

The Name Game

Joseph's Story

I believe that names have meaning, and with each of my children, we took time to pick their names with great intentionality. For example, after we had miscarried twice after our first child and then had a second child, we named her Mila. Mila is short for Milagros, which is a Spanish word meaning miracle. As doctors had told us, we might not be able to have another child. When Mila came, it was a miracle. And boy, does she live up to the name Mila Grace Small. She is a bundle of sunshine sure to make anyone's day better. Like Mila, both Aiden's and Lucy's (oldest and youngest) names have deep meaning.

That being said, having the name Joseph is significant. I believe there is a correlation between my name and being the black sheep that I am, much like Joseph in the book of Genesis. You see, if you're not familiar with Joseph, you are about to become familiar. Here is the breakdown of Joseph's life. Joseph was born to Jacob and Rachel. Back in the day, since technology wasn't around during the beginning of days, they had a lot of babies. There wasn't much else to do if you catch my drift. Joseph was his father's favorite of all the half-sons, so much so that he gave him this fancy jacket of sorts. This jacket or coat of many colors caused Joseph to become a bigger black sheep in his own family than you can imagine. Then Joseph got some dreams. Now, we all have dreams, but his dreams were very specific and audacious. The problem was that the dreams were of his brothers bowing down to him. And Joseph sure did black sheep it up by running and telling his brothers all about how they were going to bow to him. Shockingly, they didn't enjoy these dreams. So plotting as folks do, Joseph's brothers eventually ended up selling him into slavery. Now, they didn't tell their dad the truth; they went about their shenanigans and tomfoolery with outstanding excellence.

Joseph goes from being a boy whose dad loves him to a servant in a foreign land with no more special treatment. Not only does our boy Joe not get special treatment, but he eventually gets thrown in prison on a rape charge that never happened. Talk about your black sheep. But because he is a black sheep, it doesn't matter where he is. He is going to have an impact. While in prison, he begins interpreting dreams better than that of 1990s scam artist mama Cleo. This gets Joe from the dungeon to the throne room pretty quickly as the vizier of Egypt as pharaoh needs help deciphering his own dreams.

Joseph is living the quintessential black sheep life. This is the type of life that God glorifies. Joseph has made mistakes, sure. He has also been put in some crazy situations, but he always stays true to himself amid any chaos because that's what a black sheep do. Ultimately, what ends up happening is a famine hits their land, and Joseph's brothers come face to face with their bad decision. You see, what happens in the darkness, almost always seems to come to light. The original Joe Bro's bowed down, and what Joseph had dreamed had now come to fruition.

What I want you to try and understand is the emotional, mental, physical, and spiritual toll that Joseph had to endure. Yes, we see he has been obedient and faithful for certain. But can you imagine those days when Joe was alone, exhausted, and still had in his mind the dreams and promises of God? It is a very surreal place that a black sheep can get to. You truly find out the depths of who you are in those moments. At any time, any single moment, he could have quit it all. Just took those dreams, crumpled them up, and threw them away. But Joseph never did. He stayed faithful. *That* is what being a black sheep is all about. Joseph's story is just one of many heroes of faith.

Joseph was loyal, gave people grace and mercy though at times he, himself was shown none. He could have played the victim and blamed everyone else for his circumstances, but that's not what a black sheep does. Playing the victim is easy. Every one on this planet has gone through something traumatic. But we have a choice on how to respond. Black sheep are so used to hard things that they never play the "poor me game" but rather, they pick themselves up, confront the current challenge one day at a time, and move forward. I love what is called the *Serenity Prayer* in Alcoholics Anonymous. God grant me the serenity to accept the things I cannot change, the courage to change the things I can, and the wisdom to know the difference. If we can live that out, leaning on your higher power, that I choose to call God, life gets better.

Joseph trusted the promises of God. If you believe the Bible it says that God knew you before you were born. He is for you and has plans for your life. There is a stat that is thrown out in some leadership books I've read and it states that everyone, no matter your status will influence ten thousand people in their lifetime. So then my question is, how are you influencing people? What is your daily interactions with the people you do life with and those you just bump into? Are you kind to a waiter who is struggling to keep up? Do we yell at our kids more than we encourage them? Do we speak life with our words or do we speak negative/death? Joseph understood that no matter the circumstances,

He knew what God had promised and his faith carried him through some of the toughest tests a person could go through. Joseph is an O.G. Black sheep as he lived above the chaos and noise, stayed focused, kept his integrity and character intact and kept the faith, one day at a time!

S- Stop and pause. Let's take a minute to truly connect with what we read and felt.

_____

H-Heart connection. What is something unique that stood out from the previous section, what touched your heart and why?

_____

E-Explain how you can use this as a positive force for change in your daily life. Write it out.

_____

E-Examine yourself to see if there's anything else you want to write. (Your healing story is what is used to change others. God turns all brokenness to goodness for His purpose)

_____

P-Pray towards your purpose. Pray and meditate. Focus on openness and boldness to use the gifts and talents that make you who you are everyday!

Chapter 9

I Noah guy

Having survived Hurricane Harvey, I can honestly say that I have seen a good storm. Now what I can't say is that I built a boat big enough to carry two of every imaginable creature, except the dinosaurs, but we're not going to get into dinosaurs here. But could you imagine T-rex chilling on a boat? I digress. Noah is a verified black sheep if there ever was one. Noah black sheeped so hard that it truly set the bar for all other black sheep. Noah heard from God that soon it was going to rain so hard and so bad that everything was going to be wiped out except, of course, those that were going to hang out on his ark. So one day, Noah has to try and convince people that water is going to start falling from the sky. Because before that day, there is no record of it ever raining! As if Noah's task wasn't audacious enough to build a huge boat, now he had to tell people the very thing they were mocking him about had the potential to save them. But Noah and all of us black sheep know that other sheep are unwilling to stop their mocking and laughing because that's what "everyone else was doing." Noah stood out, was lonely and hard-working, and gave it his best to tell people, but "you can't cure stupid." But I digress.

Not only does Noah have to convince people water is going to drop from the heavens, but it's not going to stop until everything is wiped out, including them. I don't know what type of friends you hang around, but mine and I can tell some jokes. We can get to giggling like nobody's business, but none of my friends has ever come and proclaimed anything near as outrageous as Noah did to his buddies.

Of course, Noah got ostracized. Water falling from the sky is a tough sell on its own merits, but then to add a zoo into the equation, psh, good luck. Noah just got to work like black sheep do and began crafting an ark so glorious that it could withstand any torrential downpour. The day came when the first drop of rain fell from the sky. Man alive, how awesome would it have been to see Noah's face when that happened? Of course, it would probably quickly switch to some concern considering now he had to load a bunch of wild animals into a contraption none of them could have truly enjoyed being in. I imagine the people of that day were very similar to the people in Houston when Harvey was out in the gulf just hanging out. People would tell me all the time it's not going to hit us, or some version of it's not going to be a big deal. It's astonishing how wrong people can be yet how boldly they can make their predictions.

Now look, the Old Testament text says Noah did all this while he was six hundred years old and in Jewish tradition they say that it took him one hundred and twenty years to build. Personally having struggled to ever successfully build even a home out of "Lincoln logs" as a kid, I can imagine something that big took some time. It wasn't like Noah had some "Tim the Tool man Taylor" power tools. He had to keep the faith of what God spoke to him at an astounding age and put his head down and build.

When hurricane Harvey hit us in Houston, it dropped fifty six inches of rain and that amount, and the wind damage, changed life dramatically. Life pauses as you have to rebuild and pray some of your prized possessions have survived the storm. Being from Las Vegas, I hadn't seen fifty six inches of rain cumulatively over the course of my life, let alone over the course of five days. But I do want to give a shout out to the mini Noahs in Houston who figured out that a refrigerator floats. Yep, that's right, folks were ripping the doors off their fridge and using it as a boat to get to dry land. Loved the ingenuity and creativity of people just to survive.

So you can imagine what Noah dealt with. He spent one hundred and twenty years hearing sarcastic jokes from friends asking "Hey, when's this flood gonna show up"? Or "You built that boat so far from water its basically an extravagant pet hotel, way ahead of its time". Ok, the last one is ridiculous, but you get the point. Noah was so different because God had a specific plan for his life. So do YOU!

We all know the end of Noah's story and how God promised never to flood the earth like that again. But what is your takeaway from Noah's story? Because I guarantee that there are similarities between your story and Noah's if you are a black sheep, whether it's his love of his fellow man, his stubbornness, his work ethic, his hatred of the dinosaurs, or whatever! Don't you see yourself in Noah? Then perhaps a man after God's own heart will do the trick.

S- Stop and pause. Let's take a minute to truly connect with what we read and felt.

_____

H-Heart connection. What is something unique that stood out from the previous section, what touched your heart and why?

_____

E-Explain how you can use this as a positive force for change in your daily life. Write it out.

_____

E-Examine yourself to see if there's anything else you want to write. (Your healing story is what is used to change others. God turns all brokenness to goodness for His purpose)

_____

P-Pray towards your purpose. Pray and meditate. Focus on openness and boldness to use the gifts and talents that make you who you are everyday!

Chapter 10

Dirty Jobs

I'm not saying I have had the best of jobs in my life. They've been pretty awesome, especially working for the Raiders, but none of my jobs included things like fighting off lions and bears in the job description. Also, I know we have established that the modern human doesn't really have a grasp on being a shepherd. It's just not one of those careers that come up on career day at school. Shepherding has to be a lonely job. Look, I like sheep as much as the next guy, but I'm not trying to spend my weekends with a flock of soon-to-be ugly Christmas sweaters.

Our next hero of faith happens to be one of, if not *the* greatest shepherd of all time. Calm down, Bible quiz folks, I know Jesus was called the good shepherd and is the greatest, get off my back. Not only is shepherding hard and lonely, but our hero David also has to worry about his brothers. It has to be downright miserable. Being the best at a lot of things is lonely. David is the name of our next black sheep. David is a young man who is anointed to be the next King of Israel despite the fact that the current king had a son the same age as David. A fact that would cause David, a black sheep, years of suffering at the hands of King Saul. Now, David is truly one of the greatest leaders in the history of the world. Many know of his triumph over Goliath, but they don't dive much deeper into his life than that. I don't blame them. Have you ever tried to use a slingshot? Let alone use it to save your life and kill a giant that is threatening your family and all your friends' families. But I digress. After that resounding victory, David goes on a black sheep journey that will be remembered throughout the ages.

David is so talented that the generation above him, Saul, gets jealous. Have you ever had someone become jealous of you? And I'm not talking jealousy like a kid's-jealous-their-brother-got-slightly-more-ice-cream-than-them type of jealousy. I'm talking homicidal-rage jealousy. Like Jerry-Springer, "He is not the father"-in-the-nineties jealousy! Let me tell you, it's not a fun place to be. Being a black sheep isn't easy. It's not the fun you hear of. David learns this pretty quickly as he is run out of the palace, runs out of town, and has to hide in caves for a bit until an old man's jealousy can be curtailed.

Then a day comes when David has the opportunity of a lifetime. He has snuck over to the enemies' camp and is standing right over Saul, who is dead asleep. He could literally take a kill shot with his spear and end all of his troubles in one move. But this is so critical, you see, black sheep don't seek vengeance. Sure, they have every right to want justice, but the beauty of the black sheep is that the black sheep does just enough to send a warning shot but not get in the way of God's hand. I want to focus right here because this is where you see the true DNA of a black sheep. He shows mercy when most would have chosen vengeance. Many sheep lack the capacity for emotions like empathy. But you and I, as black sheep, get David here because we can relate to his empathy! Empathy is such an underrated and overlooked characteristic in our world today. True leaders are empathetic leaders.

This sets the tone for David's black-sheep life. David's story after that moment continues to be filled with ups and downs. His story, though, is all of our stories. There are mountaintop seasons where things are incredible, and then there are valley seasons. The one thing that is constant is change. Let me say this, in a mountain range when you look at it, all the life is at the bottom, nearest the valley where there is always growth and life taking place. The mountaintop is usually rocky and has less life going on. It's quiet and almost lonely. Life is bigger than just the mountaintop highs and experiences. Yes enjoy those great moments in life, but understand black sheep that if you can figure out how to thrive in the valley, you will live a fulfilled and joyful life. Because it isn't about the highs or lows of life, it's the journey and process and who is walking with you in each season of life. We get so caught up in trying to capture moments on our phones these days that we aren't living in each moment and enjoying the life all around us. Black sheep learn to be present because they value time with other sheep.

David was a complicated man with a lot going on throughout his life. David, the man after God's own heart, would later go on to break God's heart. Yet God never fails David despite David failing Him. The promises God made to David came true. I promise you that even though you and I will never be kings of Israel, we share a common bond with David, for we are black sheep.

S- Stop and pause. Let's take a minute to truly connect with what we read and felt.

H-Heart connection. What is something unique that stood out from the previous section, what touched your heart and why?

E-Explain how you can use this as a positive force for change in your daily life. Write it out.

E-Examine yourself to see if there's anything else you want to write. (Your healing story is what is used to change others. God turns all brokenness to goodness for His purpose)

P-Pray towards your purpose. Pray and meditate. Focus on openness and boldness to use the gifts and talents that make you who you are everyday!

Chapter 11

Hall of Faith

The Old Testament and New Testament alike are filled with stories of black sheep. Hebrews goes on to list what I like to call the "hall of faith," which is a list of individuals listed in the eleventh chapter who are all black sheep. It lists people like Abel, Enoch, Noah, Abraham, and Sarah. All of these biblical heroes fit the mold of the black sheep. The book of Hebrews even calls them foreigners because they were so different. The New Testament also records stories of the black sheep. Jesus picks a cadre of black sheep to be his inner circle, twelve of them to be exact. What's remarkable is that even among the group of black sheep, there were black sheep. Case in point, Peter. Peter is famously known for letting his mouth and actions run out a bit in front of his brain. Whether it is denying knowing Jesus or using his sword to lop off the ear of a soldier coming for Jesus, Peter is a quintessential black sheep. After Jesus' time, possibly the greatest black sheep that the New Testament records are a man who is credited with penning most of the New Testament. You guessed it—we're talking about Paul. Paul is brilliant, bold, and one hundred percent black sheep. He starts his career as a man who kills Christians. Not only does he kill them, but he also organizes groups of people to gather together and throw rocks at someone until they die. Not that I'm ranking ways to die, but that has to be in the top ten of the worst ways to meet our maker.

Paul then is on his way to a town called Damascus and has an encounter with God that reshapes his life. Paul radically reverses course and becomes one of the greatest advocates for Christ ever. Paul is ostracized by his past friends, and his new friends are rightfully a bit wary of him. He spends a whole lot of his life in prisons and under great stress, as most black sheep do. While in prison, he writes many letters to churches all around the world, which become some of the most influential writings in the history of the world. The black sheep have this incredible ability to produce and excel in the face of tremendous adversity that causes others to wilt.

Paul truly embodies the spirit of the black sheep and is someone who the history books, including the Bible, sing his praises. But again, praises aren't what the black sheep care about. Actually, they make the black sheep uncomfortable. Praises are truly only meant for One. The black sheep produce and excel not for a taste of the glory like Nacho Libre but rather for the opportunity to be a part of the group. It is all about community for the black sheep. Black sheep thrive when together. It truly is why there are so many shepherding references throughout so many historical books. The Bible even calls Jesus the "Good Shepherd," and there's a parable about the "lost sheep." I mean, I could go on and on about the biblical parallels, but ultimately, I don't want you to get too wrapped up in all that. It's more valuable at this moment to think back to when we first started this journey together. I mentioned a hierarchy that places things in order. It's time, black sheep, for a new order of things. It's time for unity, empathy, kindness, love, joy, peace, and *everything good*! It all starts with us!

What stands out to you about the Hall of Faith? What specific things in your life help grow your faith? How do you utilize them? I encourage you to pray, meditate, and even journal about this!

Conclusion

There are so many leadership lessons, thoughts, or parables regarding sheep and shepherds that the market is saturated. While some of them are good stuff, others just are flat-out untrue and manipulative. Don't believe me? Allow me to demystify one of the biggest lies told to young leaders, especially those pursuing ministry. There is this story of how oftentimes, a shepherd who has a sheep that strays from the flock will break the sheep's legs and then carry the sheep while it heals to teach it a lesson. If you've never heard this, I promise your pastor/priest knows it. The problem with this story is that it is completely ridiculous. It has been proven that shepherds have much better things to do and better strategies than having to carry a sheep around. Sadly, this story is used by manipulative leaders to try and control young sheep who are starting to flourish.

Now is the time for us black sheep to unite and let our voices and, more importantly, our actions be heard. It is time to use our God-given skill sets together to help heal the world God gave us before it's too late. We live in a broken world with broken people. However, for far too long, the black sheep among us have stood alone, not knowing how to use our gifts and talents to make a difference.

I wish I could tell you that everything will magically get better. But as black sheep, we don't lie to one another, so I won't. But what I can tell you is from my experience, opening up and sharing, using the things society has overlooked in my life as a force for good, has made a tremendous impact on my life. Am I still hurting? Yes. Are there still bad days? Of course! But I have found that the more I tell and share my story, the more other people begin to open up to me. It's as if by sharing our stories, no matter how big or small or even if it's sharing a small part of what we have been through, but by sharing, healing happens.

Just as brutally open and honest as I was, in the beginning, is how brutally honest I will be with you now. Allow me to share how I go through a typical day. How that plays out in my life is simply this: I wake up. I take some time to pray, read, and meditate. I work out (not nearly as much as I should). I shower, eat, and then make a few important phone calls every morning, touching base with family and/or friends. Then I go to work. Then I go to a meeting (AA, three to five times a week). Go home. Watch something (usually sports or some trending show/movie). Eat. More phone calls. Sleep. Repeat. Pretty much every day. Routine is not the end all be all for a black sheep, though it's important. Is my life where I want it to be? Not even close. I sit here today in a sober living home, having lost my dad to a heart attack just a year and a half ago, with three kidney stones, a few amazing friends, divorced, co-parenting the most amazing kids, with an amazing girlfriend working on blending families, one side of my family having rocky relationships with me, an incredible mom—you know all the fun perks of black sheeping. Would I change any of it? Fuck, no. I love my life. But like you, my black sheep friend, I'm just getting started! So let's get out there. The world desperately needs all of us, unified, using every single bit of our black sheepness. Thank you for taking the time to read this. I'm humbled you did. Share the book with a friend. I also encourage you, black sheep, to open up, find your flock, and be as black sheep as you want to be. Never change. You are exactly who you are supposed to be at this exact moment. Can we grow? You bet your ass we can. But never let anyone tell you you should be ashamed of any part of who you are. Love you, black sheep. —Joe

Index

Printed by Amazon Italia Logistica S.r.l.
Torrazza Piemonte (TO), Italy